Introduction

A complete history of piracy would fill many volumes. Pirates have always been with us in one form or another, from the prehistoric sea rovers of the Bronze Age to the present-day river pirates of some East Asian ports—mainly maritime burglars who board and pilfer from ships lying at anchor during the night.

Popular misconceptions of the appearance of the old-time pirates have been encouraged by fanciful illustrations in books and magazines and the swashbuckling apparitions of the films and stage who bear little resemblance to the historic figures.

Vikings, for instance, are popularly portrayed as wrapped in furs and wearing huge horned or winged helmets. This was the dress, perhaps, of warriors of the Bronze Age, but the Norse marauders actually looked quite different.

The buccaneers of the Spanish Main in the seventeenth century were a colorful and eccentric crew of cutthroats of many races and nationalities. Though many sported jewelry and wore fine silks and brocades plundered from their victims, on the whole they wore the clothing of seamen and gentlemen of the period, depending upon their rank aboard ship.

Privateers were armed private vessels commissioned by a warring power to cruise against the fleet and commerce of an enemy nation. In actuality, the privateersmen of the seventeenth century were often professional pirates in peacetime who were enlisted into the service of a belligerent nation as a convenience, with few questions asked. Privateering, because of the often handsome profits involved in prize money, was a very popular avocation during the wars of the seventeenth and eighteenth centuries. During the American Revolution many a young man evaded or deserted service in the Continental army by signing aboard a privateer.

I am currently working as an underwater illustrator and historical researcher on the site of a sunken Spanish galleon of the seventeenth century located off Walker Cay in the northern Bahama Islands. There is reason to suspect that this ship may have been plundered and sunk by one of the many pirate vessels that infested the Bahamas during the period when the great Spanish treasure fleets annually sailed home to Spain from the New World.

The drawings in this book were composed, after much research, from original pictures done in the seventeenth, eighteenth and nineteenth centuries, or from written descriptions contemporary or nearly contemporary with the actual people and events. Despite the wonderfully colorful depictions of these corsairs by many illustrators of the last hundred years, I was unable to find any early pictures or descriptions of pirates or buccaneers wearing wooden legs, eye patches, earrings or kerchiefs bound about their heads, or carrying parrots on their shoulders.

All the pictures appear in color on the covers for the guidance of those who wish to use authentic coloring in the book.

PETER F. COPELAND

Peter F. Copeland

PIRATES and BUCCANEERS
Coloring Book

Dover Publications, Inc.

New York

To Moira

Published in Canada by General Publishing Company,
Ltd., 30 Lesmill Road, Don Mills, Toronto, Ontario.
Published in the United Kingdom by Constable and Com-
pany, Ltd.

Pirates and Buccaneers Coloring Book is a new work,
first published by Dover Publications, Inc., in 1977.

International Standard Book Number: 0-486-23393-6

Manufactured in the United States of America
Dover Publications, Inc.
180 Varick Street
New York, N. Y. 10014

1. Viking Raider, 795 A.D. The Viking sea rovers of the period 795 A.D. through the beginning of the eleventh century attacked and plundered coastal settlements and towns all over the British Isles and northern France, eventually establishing Scandinavian kingdoms in England and Normandy. In fact, the Vikings did not wear great horned or winged helmets, nor did they wrap themselves in the skins of animals. These were the trappings of the Bronze Age, of many centuries before. Viking dress was simple and functional, as were Viking weapons.

2. Stertebeker, a Hanseatic Pirate in the North Sea, 1392. Stertebeker was one of the best known of the German pirates of the Baltic and North Seas in the days of the Hanseatic League of German seaports. One of a pirate band known as "The Friends of God and the Enemies of the World," he captured many trading vessels in northern waters, and participated in the sack and burning of Bergen in Norway in 1392. The ship in the background is a carrack of the late fourteenth century.

3. A French Filibuster, 1550. The filibusters of France (*flibustiers:* freebooters, in French) made their base on the island of Guerino near Honduras in the 1530s. In small vessels they attacked the large Spanish galleons in the Caribbean, making off with great wealth. In 1555 the filibusters sacked the city of Havana, remaining there for three weeks, and leaving with an immense amount of treasure. The ship is a small sixteenth-century Spanish coasting vessel used in South American waters.

4. An English Pirate in the Pacific, 1587. Captain Thomas Cavendish attacked the rich Spanish Manila galleons in the Pacific and raided the coastal towns of Mexico, returning to England just after the defeat of the Spanish Armada in 1588.

5. Khair-ed-Din Barbarossa, a Turkish Pirate in the Mediterranean, Sixteenth Century. Khair-ed-Din, one of the fierce Barbarossa brothers, cruised the Barbary Coast for the Sultan of Turkey during the sixteenth century. In Europe, at the very mention of his name, "men swore, and women crossed themselves."

6. An English Privateersman with Sir Richard Hawkins at Valparaiso, 1594. Sir Richard Hawkins set off as a privateersman aboard his ship the *Dainty*, sailing through the Straits of Magellan, and plundered the port of Valparaiso, Chile, in 1594. The privateersman shown here fights with dagger and rapier, Elizabethan fashion. The ship is a late sixteenth-century English vessel.

7. A Dutch Soldier of Admiral van Speilbergen at Salagua, Mexico, 1615. The Dutch freebooters raided Spanish shipping and settlements on the Pacific coast of Latin America in six expeditions between 1599 and 1643. Admiral van Speilbergen commanded one such raid in 1615 which led to a pitched battle with Spanish forces at Salagua, Mexico. The soldier shown here carries a heavy matchlock musket, fired by a burning fuse or slow match, which he carries between his fingers, and supported in a forked rest used for aiming.

8. A "Boucanier" of Hispaniola, 1655. The original buccaneers were hunters on the island of Hispaniola in the Caribbean, and were so called from the *boucan,* the grill made of green wood over which they smoked their meat. These poor and tattered hunters were attracted to a life of sea roving by the richly laden Spanish treasure ships that annually sailed through the Caribbean.

9. An English Pirate, 1650. Spain, England, France and Holland were so continually involved in wars with one another during the second half of the seventeenth century that the distinction between pirate and privateersman became very thin indeed. Captains like the Englishman shown here often received letters of marque from their governments commissioning them to attack the enemy in wartime. Upon the return of peace they reverted to piracy, attacking any vessel they came across.

10. Henry Morgan, a Buccaneer of Jamaica, 1675. A Welshman, Henry Morgan was transported as a servant to Barbados in his youth. Serving as a soldier of fortune and privateersman, Morgan gained a great reputation, raiding the Dutch islands and the Spanish settlements in America. In 1668 Morgan was appointed colonel of freebooters, and raided Puerto Príncipe and Portobello in Panama, returning to Jamaica with an immense haul of booty. Morgan and his men took the city of Maracaibo in 1669, and in 1671 stormed Panama City and gained another rich haul in treasure. In later years Morgan was knighted by the King of England and returned to Jamaica as Lieutenant Governor in 1674. He died peacefully in bed, a wealthy planter, in 1688. A Spanish galleon is in the background.

11. A Spanish Pirate in the Caribbean, 1640. The riches of the Spanish treasure fleets sailing from America lured adventurers and desperados from all over Europe to the West Indies. By the mid-seventeenth century they formed a pirate confederacy called "The Brothers of the Coast," among whom were Spaniards, Frenchmen, Englishmen, Dutchmen, Portuguese, Indians and blacks. The ship is an English galleon.

12. One of Henry Morgan's Buccaneers at Portobello, 1668. The Spanish stronghold of Portobello in Panama was attacked and plundered by Henry Morgan, chief of the English privateers of Jamaica, in 1668. A quarter of a million pieces of eight, as well as much other booty, was carried back to Port Royal, Jamaica, by men such as this ragged buccaneer.

13. Bartolomew Portugues, a Pirate in the Caribbean, 1669. One of the group of desperate men who preyed upon the rich Spanish treasure galleons of the Caribbean, this Portuguese pirate operated mainly in the waters off Campeche, Mexico. The ship is a lateen-rigged Caribbean island trader of the seventeenth century.

14. Rock Brasiliano, a Caribbean Pirate, 1670. Born a Dutchman, Rock was nicknamed "Brasiliano" because of his long residence in Brazil. He hated the Spanish fiercely, and was accused of awful cruelties perpetrated upon Spanish prisoners, including roasting them on wooden spits. In the background is a seventeenth-century merchant ship.

15. Captain John Avery, a Madagascar Pirate, 1695. "Long Ben" Avery, called "The Arch Pyrat," captured the treasure ship of the Great Mogul of India, one of the prizes of which was the Great Mogul's daughter, whom Long Ben gallantly carried off to Madagascar and married. Despite a fortune in gold and jewels taken by him during his career, Long Ben died in poverty in England in 1698.

16. Tortuga Pirates Boarding a Merchantman, 1665. Tortuga pirates, known as "The Brothers of the Coast," were a rough and colorful gang of cutthroats, the terror of the Caribbean Sea.

17. Jean David Nau, Called "L'Ollonois," a French Pirate in the Caribbean, 1667. L'Ollonois rose from the life of an indentured servant in the West Indies to achieve one of the most fearsome reputations in the history of piracy and buccaneering. He looted Maracaibo and Puerto Cabello, among other exploits, but is chiefly remembered for the horrifying cruelties he vented upon captives. This fiend is once reported to have cut the heart out of a living Spanish prisoner and eaten it on the spot. Fittingly, Jean David Nau finally was captured by the Carib Indians, who devoured him and a number of his followers.

18. Pierre Le Grand, a French Buccaneer in the Caribbean, 1665. One of the most feared corsairs of Tortuga, Pierre Le Grand once captured a great Spanish galleon with a small boatload of buccaneers armed only with swords and pistols. The ship is a Dutch East Indiaman of the seventeenth century.

19. Jean Bart, a French Privateersman in the North Sea, 1695. Jean Bart was perhaps the most famous of the French privateersmen of the seventeenth century, and a hero of the French navy. His lightning raids on the English coast destroyed much English shipping.

20. Captain William Kidd, 1698. Probably the best remembered of all pirates who sailed the seas, William Kidd was only a mediocre pirate, who was plagued by bad luck. He was tried in England, found guilty of piracy and murder, and hanged on May 23, 1701. In the background is a French ship of the first rate, 108 guns, of the late seventeenth century.

21. Captain Regnier Tongrelow, a New York Privateersman in the Caribbean, 1706. Much of the sea wealth of the colony of New York came to it through its privateersmen, who, during the wars with the French, brought home many rich prizes. Regnier Tongrelow, who commanded the New York galley in 1706, was a well-known privateersman who had "all of the makings of a pirate inside his privateering veneer."

22. Edward Teach, Alias "Blackbeard," 1718. Perhaps the most ferocious pirate of the Spanish Main, Blackbeard, after a bloody career, was killed in battle at Okracoke Inlet, North Carolina, in 1718. His head was cut off and fixed to the bowsprit of the vessel that took him. In the background is a Spanish treasure ship at Vigo Bay.

23. Anne Bonny, an English Pirate, 1724. Both Anne Bonny and her shipmate Mary Read were "fair to look upon," as the old books have it. Anne Bonny, an Irish girl, grew up in Carolina, and ran away with a sailor at a tender age. She was swept off her feet by the picturesque and impetuous "Calico Jack" Rackham, and went away with him on his pirate forays. When Rackham's crew were surprised and attacked by an armed sloop, she fought gallantly until made prisoner. Tried for piracy at Jamaica, and convicted, Anne pleaded pregnancy, and her sentence was commuted. Nothing is known of her eventual fate.

24. Mary Read, an English Pirate, 1724. Mary Read, disguising herself as a male, served from her youth as footboy, sailor, soldier and pirate. Captured by pirates from New Providence in the Bahamas, Mary joined them, delighting in life among the rough sea robbers. She served aboard the ship of "Calico Jack" Rackham, where she met Anne Bonny. Eventually captured, Mary was sentenced to be hanged, but died of a fever soon after. The ship is a French galliot, or ketch, of the eighteenth century.

25. Captain John Smith, Alias "Captain Gow," Hanged in England, 1725. Smith would seem to have been a Scotsman, from his dress and weapons. He carried a Highland-style sword and a Highland shield, or targ. He raided off the coast of Spain and was executed in England in 1725.

26. Captain Bartholomew Roberts, 1722. One of the outstanding pirates of the eighteenth century, Captain Roberts took over 400 ships along the Guinea coast and in the West Indies. His customary dress was "a rich damask waistcoat and breeches, and a gold chain round his neck with a large diamond cross dangling from it." Roberts was killed in battle in 1722 and was thrown overboard by his crew, fully armed and richly attired.

27. "Calico Jack" Rackham, 1720. Known as "Calico Jack" because of the shirt and breeches of calico that he habitually wore, Captain John Rackham commanded the pirate ship aboard which Mary Read and Anne Bonny served. He was hanged at Gallow's Point, Jamaica, in 1720. Anne Bonny is reported to have said of him, "If he had fought like a man, he need not have been hanged like a dog."

28. Captain John Quelch, Hanged at Boston, 1704. In the summer of 1703 the crew of the Boston privateer *Charles* took over their ship. They threw the captain overboard, and elected the young John Quelch to command them on a pirate cruise. They plundered Portuguese ships on the coast of Brazil for a year before returning to Marblehead, Massachusetts, with a load of booty. Arrested and clapped into jail in Boston, they were tried and sentenced to be hanged for piracy in 1704.

29. Stede Bonnet, a Pirate on the Carolina Coast, 1717. Major Stede Bonnet, once a planter in Barbados, became a pirate, it is said, to escape a nagging wife. With his ship *Revenge* he joined Blackbeard, and preyed upon coastwise shipping off the Carolinas. Bonnet was tried and hanged at Charleston in 1718. The ship is an English East Indiaman of the eighteenth century.

30. An American Privateer Captain, 1760. The French and Indian War again saw American privateersmen assisting the British fleet in battle against the French. Seen in his shoregoing finery, this captain wears a blue coat which emulates the frock coat of an officer of the Royal Navy. He toasts his good fortune in prize money with a wooden tankard of Colonial rum.

31. Captain Ned Low, an English Pirate, 1720. An immigrant lad who came to Boston, Ned Low went to sea and turned pirate. He was a cruel and ruthless foe who delighted in torturing captives before killing them. Cast adrift by his crew in 1724, he was picked up by a French ship and hanged at Martinique.

32. Gun Crew of an American Privateer, 1777. Privateers, during the American Revolution, promised adventure and the possibility of large profits in prize money to many a man who wished to avoid service in the hard-pressed, ill-fed Continental army. Privateers' crews were composed of many races and nationalities. Blacks, Europeans and Indians commonly served together aboard these vessels.

33. Captain James Mugford, an American Privateersman, 1776. Captain Mugford commanded the privateer schooner *Franklin* of Marblehead, Massachusetts, and was killed in May 1776. The captain wears an outfit copied from the uniform of an officer of the Continental navy, as did a number of privateer captains in American service.

34. An American Privateersman, 1780. Swarms of American privateers harassed the British at sea throughout the Revolution. The damage done to England's maritime commerce is estimated to have been over eighteen million dollars. This Yankee sailor wears a navy cutlass and carries a boarding pike.

35. James Ryder Mowat, a Loyalist Privateersman, 1779. James Ryder Mowat commanded an armed cruiser in the British service during the Revolution. He is described in a newspaper advertisement of the time as wearing a short green coat trimmed with narrow gold lace, striped trousers and a fur cap. In the background is an eighteenth-century frigate.

36. Gustavus Conyngham, an American Privateersman, 1777. Over two thousand American privateers preyed upon British shipping during the Revolution. Among the most famous privateer captains, Gustavus Conyngham was called by the British "the pirate of Dunkirk."

37. Captain of a French Privateer, 1797. Many French privateers during the period of the French Revolutionary government operated against British shipping. A great number were based at Charleston, South Carolina, which city profited greatly from the activities of these French sea raiders.

38. A French Privateersman, 1797. France and Britain fought on land and sea from about 1792 through 1815. Whereas the navy of Revolutionary France was no match for the British fleet, French privateersmen operated successfully against British shipping for many years. In the background is the French frigate *La Pomone*.

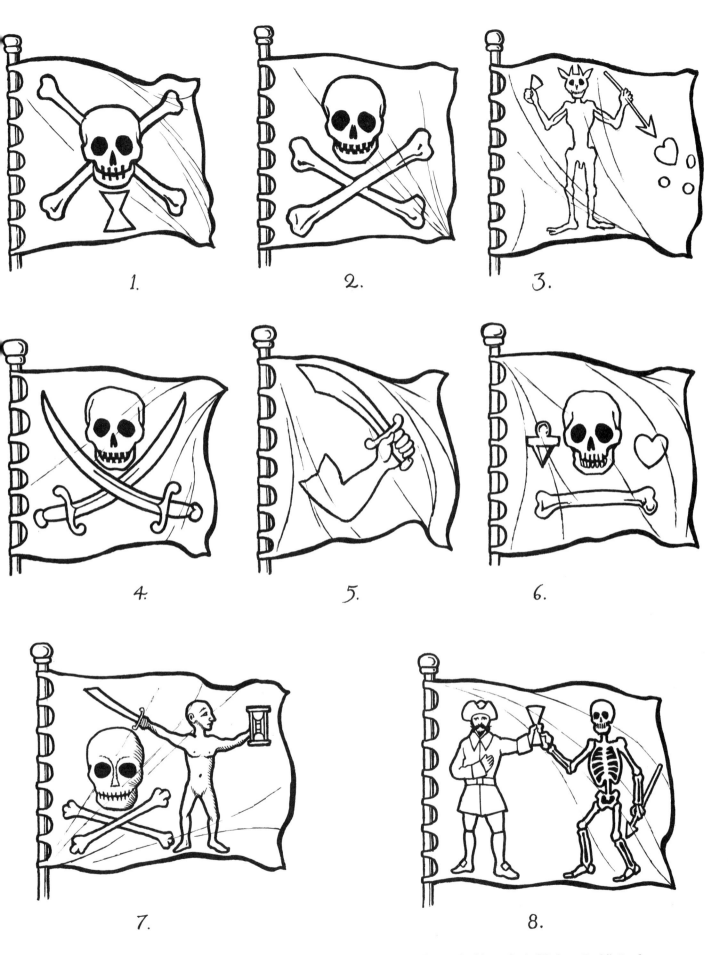

39. Flags of Pirates. 1. French filibusters. 2. Captain England. 3. Blackbeard. 4. "Calico Jack" Rackham. 5. Captain Thomas Tew. 6. Stede Bonnet. 7. French pirate ship *Sanspitié*. 8. Captain Bartholomew Roberts.

40. An Algerian Pirate, 1800. Pirates had infested the North African coast since the days of Barbarossa. Between 1569 and 1616 the Algerian corsair fleet had taken 469 British ships at sea, some in English home waters. The crews of these ill-fated vessels were sold into slavery. Finally the young United States took action to end the menace of the Barbary pirates, who by 1800 were receiving tributary payments from nine European nations. A declaration of war by Tripoli was followed in 1804 by an American invasion, and in June 1805 a treaty was signed stipulating that no more American vessels would be attacked by the pirates of the Barbary Coast. Finally, between 1816 and 1820, the nations of Europe brought piracy to an end on the coast of North Africa.

41. Jean Lafitte, a Pirate in the Gulf of Mexico and the West Indies, 1809. Jean Lafitte operated in the Gulf of Mexico and the West Indies from 1809 until about 1820. Lafitte allied himself and his crew with the Americans under General Andrew Jackson and fought at the Battle of New Orleans in 1815. This picture is based upon a portrait of Lafitte in the Louisiana State Museum.

42. An American Privateersman, 1812. Fast-sailing American privateers such as the *Bunker Hill* and the *Trueblooded Yankee* swarmed over the seas in 1812, making prizes of British ships. Within six months 300 prizes had been taken by United States vessels, both naval and privateer.

43. Charles Gibbs, a Caribbean Pirate, 1818. It is related that Captain Charles Gibbs, upon capturing a young Dutch girl, defended her against his own crew, but later permitted her to be poisoned. Gibbs was hanged for murder in New York in 1838. In the background is a barquentine that has struck her colors.

44. A Spanish Pirate from the *Panda*, 1832. The last publicized act of piracy in American waters occurred in 1832, when the United States brig *Mexican* was taken in the North Atlantic by the Spanish pirate ship *Panda*, commanded by Don Pedro Gibert. Eleven men of the *Panda's* crew were eventually tried in Boston, and five of the pirates were hanged in America's last execution for piracy in 1835. The brig *Mexican* is in the background.